mark

A DOUBLE-EDGED BIBLE STUDY

NAVPRESS

Discipleship Inside Out™

TH1NK: **Life**Change™

NAVPRESS ⬤

Discipleship Inside Out™

NavPress is the publishing ministry of The Navigators, an international Christian organization and leader in personal spiritual development. NavPress is committed to helping people grow spiritually and enjoy lives of meaning and hope through personal and group resources that are biblically rooted, culturally relevant, and highly practical.

For a free catalog go to www.NavPress.com
or call 1.800.366.7788 in the United States or 1.800.839.4769 in Canada.

www.navpress.com

TH1NK and the TH1NK logo are registered trademarks of NavPress. Absence of ® in connection with marks of NavPress or other parties does not indicate an absence of registration of those marks.

ISBN 978-1-57683-692-7

Cover design by Arvid Wallen
Creative Team: Gabe Filkey, Eric Johnson, Nicci Jordan, Arvid Wallen, Amy Spencer, Darla Hightower, Glynese Northam

Unless otherwise identified, all Scripture quotations in this publication are taken from the HOLY BIBLE: NEW INTERNATIONAL VERSION® (NIV®). Copyright © 1973, 1978, 1984 by International Bible Society. Used by permission of Zondervan Publishing House. All rights reserved. Other versions used include: THE MESSAGE (MSG). Copyright © 1993, 1994, 1995, 1996, 2000, 2001, 2002. Used by permission of NavPress Publishing Group.

Printed in the United States of America

3 4 5 6 7 8 9 10 / 15 14 13 12 11 10

contents

introduction to TH1NK: LifeChange

Double-Edged and Ready for Action

For the word of God is living and active. Sharper than any double-edged sword, it penetrates even to dividing soul and spirit, joints and marrow; it judges the thoughts and attitudes of the heart.

Hebrews 4:12

a reason to study

Studying the Bible is more than homework. It is more than reading a textbook. And it is more than an opportunity for a social gathering. Like Hebrews suggests, the Bible knows us, challenges us, and yes, judges us. Like a double-edged sword, it's sharp enough to cut through our layers of insecurity and pretense to change our lives forever.

Deep down, isn't that what we want – to actually *experience* God's power in our lives, through Scripture? That's what TH1NK: LifeChange is all about. The purpose of this Bible study is to connect you intimately with God's Word. It can change you, not only intellectually, but also spiritually, emotionally, maybe even physically. God's Word is that powerful.

The psalmist wrote,

> *What you say goes, GOD,*
> *and* stays, *as permanent as the heavens.*
> *Your truth never goes out of fashion;*
> *it's as up-to-date as the earth when the sun comes*
> *up. . . .*
> *If your revelation hadn't delighted me so,*
> *I would have given up when the hard times came.*
> *But I'll never forget the advice you gave me;*
> *you saved my life with those wise words.*
> *Save me! I'm all yours.*
> *I look high and low for your words of wisdom.*
> *The wicked lie in ambush to destroy me,*
> *but I'm only concerned with your plans for me.*
> *I see the limits to everything human,*
> *but the horizons can't contain your commands.*
>
> (PSALM 119:89-90,92-96, MSG)

Do you notice the intimate connection the psalmist has with God *because* of the greatness of the Word? He trusts God, he loves Him, and his greatest desire is to obey. But the only way he knows how to do any of this is because he knows God's voice, God's words.

the details

Each TH1NK: LifeChange study covers one book of the Bible so you can concentrate on its particular, essential details. Although every study exclusively covers a different book, there are common threads throughout the series. Each study will do the following:

1. Help you understand the book you're studying so well that it affects your daily thinking
2. Teach valuable Bible study skills you can use on your own to go even deeper into God's Word
3. Provide a contextual understanding of the book, offering historical background, word definitions, and explanatory notes
4. Allow you to understand the message of the book as a whole
5. Demonstrate how God's Word can transform you into a bona fide representative of Jesus

Every week, plan on spending about thirty to forty-five minutes on your own to complete the study. Then get together with your group. Depending on the amount of time it takes, you can either go through a whole or a half lesson each week. If you do one lesson per week, you'll finish the study in three months. But it's all up to you.

the structure

The twelve lessons include the following elements:

Study. First you'll study the book by yourself. This is where you'll answer questions, learn cultural and biographical information, and ask God some questions of your own.

Live. After you've absorbed the information, you'll want to look in a mirror—figuratively, that is. Think about your life in the context of what you've learned. This is a time to be honest with yourself and with God about who you are and how you are living.

Connect. You know that a small-group study time isn't just for hanging out and drinking soda. A small group provides accountability and support. It's one thing to say to yourself, *I'm really going to work on this* and entirely another thing to say it to a group of your friends. Your friends can support your decisions, encourage you to follow through, and pray for you regularly. And vice versa.

In your group, you'll want to talk with each other about what you discovered on your own: things that went unanswered, things that challenged you, and things that changed you. Use the guidance in this section to lead your discussion. After that, pray for each other. This section will always provide targeted prayer topics for you and your group.

Go deeper. Thirsty for more? Just can't get enough? Then use the guidance in this section to explore even deeper the vastness of Scripture. It's similar to extra credit, for all the overachievers who love to learn.

Memory verse of the week. Did a particular verse make you think? Is there a verse you can't get out of your head? Write it down and memorize it. Allow God's Word to permanently brand itself in your head and your heart.

Notes. At the end of each chapter, there are some pages for notes. Use them to write notes from your group discussions, to ask questions of God or yourself, to write important verses and observations—or anything you want.

now go!

You are now ready to experience the Bible and the God of the Bible in an intense new way. So jump in headfirst. Allow the double-edged sword of Scripture to pierce your mind, your heart, your life.

Jesus, according to Mark

The gospel of Mark tells about Jesus. That's it. Like the three other Gospels, this book gives us an insider's account of Jesus' ministry – who He was, what He did, how He loved, why He died, that He rose and saved humanity. Mark's gospel is considered the most straightforward of the four: he dives right into Jesus' story, which may explain why it's the shortest gospel. Mark wanted us to understand that God isn't just some unapproachable Being in the sky, but that He spent a grueling human life on this watery planet to make it possible for us to be with Him. He came to give us abundant life – here, now, forever.

Mark's gospel allows us, in a way, to spend time with Jesus, to walk with Him in the cities and to go where He goes. As we study this book, we dive deeper into Jesus' story. We go from hanging out with Him to actually asking Him questions, conversing with Him. This gospel ushers us into the life of our Savior, and it can transform our lives.

Want to be more like Jesus? Get to know Him. Study this gospel and ask the Holy Spirit to lead you into a new experience.

the setting

Most likely, Mark was written by John Mark, a first-century Jewish follower of Christ. Because he went by his second name, Mark (or Marcus), scholars infer he was probably a Roman citizen, like the apostle Paul. Mark was pretty well-connected; his mother, Mary (not Jesus' mom, or Mary Magdalene, but another Mary altogether), was a good friend of Peter, and his cousin, Barnabas, accompanied Paul on his missionary adventures. These connections would have fed him firsthand information about Jesus' life and ministry. The late scholar, T. W. Manson, theorized that Mark was Peter's interpreter during his ministry in Rome.

Even with all these connections, it's unclear if Mark was an eye-witness to Jesus' ministry. But if Mark truly is John Mark, as many believe, he spent at least *some* time with Jesus (Mark 14:51-52 seems to imply he did). Either way, when Mark wrote, he knew what he was talking about.

mark's audience

Modern scholars almost unanimously agree that Mark's was the earliest of the four Gospels. He probably wrote the book after Peter died, but before Jerusalem fell, between AD 64 and 70. Mark likely wrote in Rome, but some say his book could have been written in Egypt or Syria.

It is clear, however, that Mark was written for Gentiles, or non-Jews. Mark revealed certain signs to point us toward this conclusion; for example, he explained Jewish practices, which presumes his intended audience did not already know them. Also, Mark translated Aramaic words (the Jewish language of the time) found in the text. If he were writing to Jewish people, he obviously wouldn't have needed to do that.

mark's purpose

Mark wanted to explain to his non-Jewish readers how his own people rejected Jesus – the Jewish Messiah. The Jews expected a glorious warrior king. What they got was an apparent "average Joe," a carpenter, who hung out with company not fit for a king and spoke about atypical, controversial things. It didn't make a lot of sense to a people desperately waiting for their hero to arrive. Yet supposedly they knew their Scriptures backward and forward. If they did, they should have expected their Messiah to be born of a humble birth and to live a humble, suffering life. The prophets predicted it all. But many Jews missed that part of the story.

Mark grounded his gospel in history, using trusted evidence to ensure that readers know (1) this message is true, even if the Jewish nation rejected it and (2) the gospel of Jesus is the fulfillment of God's promises through and to Israel. Christ's story can't be understood apart from its historical context.

the history of good news

Gospel is an Old English word that means "good news." It comes from the Greek word *euangelion*. *Eu* means "good" and *angelion* means "message." You can probably tell that's where we get the words *evangelist* and *angel*.

In case you encounter this later, it's important to note that Mark, Matthew, and Luke are often lumped together (and are referred to as the Synoptic Gospels). John is considered a separate gospel because, though the Synoptic Gospels closely resemble each other, John wrote a unique account.

While modern scholars generally believe Mark was written first, second-century Christian writers thought Matthew and Luke must have been written first because they are longer books. To them, Mark was just a condensed version of the real thing.

But evidence points to Mark as the first gospel:

Matthew and Luke, while longer, contain almost the entire contents of Mark. Only thirty-one of Mark's 678 verses do not show up in either Matthew or Luke.

Matthew and Luke often smooth the rough edges of Mark's choppy Greek. Matthew tends to simplify the language and Luke makes it read better stylistically. At other times, however, Matthew and Luke – especially Matthew – reproduce Mark's language verbatim.

In light of these points, we can confidently claim that Matthew and Luke had access to at least part of what Mark had already written. It appears that Mark not only wrote the first Gospel and contributed to the others, but he also invented the Gospel format.

headline news

"**Hosanna!** Blessed is he who comes in the name of the Lord!"

Mark 11:9

Throughout the ages, human beings have probably given more time and attention to questioning God's existence than to any other concern. Most people believe, both now and throughout history, that there is a divine Being out there – somewhere – watching over us. To announce that God exists is not particularly breaking news.

But claiming that God is here, right now, right next to us – that is big news. Again, while many believe there is a God, fewer accept His role in their lives. Humans often ask of God: *Does He care about us? Pay attention to us? Torture us?* In his gospel, Mark answers those questions by introducing us to Jesus Christ. There is a God, and He does more than just watch over us. Mark gives us the opportunity to meet Him, to get to know Him, and to rely on Him completely. This is the sort of headline news that changes lives.

1 Before you dive into your study of the gospel of Mark, read it. First, read it as though it is a novel – give it your full attention and don't stop until you finish the book. Then go back and skim it and use the space below to jot down the following:

Your first impressions

Repeated words or phrases

General themes

What you discover about Jesus

Your favorite character. Least favorite

Your favorite miracle

Your own explanation of one parable

Christ. This comes from the Greek word *christos*, which **fyi** means "anointed one." It's a translation of the Hebrew word mashiach, which means "Messiah." In the Old Testament, the kings of Israel were anointed with oil as a sign of spiritual authority. The oil represented the Spirit of God.

***Son of God.* This title was not used in the Old Testament in** **fyi** reference to the coming Messiah. Instead it referred to the people of Israel or the king of Israel. It inferred ideas both of being chosen (like God's people) and of deserving obedience (like a king). Once Jesus arrived on the scene, it started being used for the Messiah.

2 What do Mark's first words (1:1) imply his gospel will be about?

3 What do Jesus' first words in Mark suggest will be the main theme of His preaching (1:15)?

live

4 What resonated with you most as you read through this book? Explain why.

5 Write down some things you'd like to learn from this twelve-week study, and how you would like your life to be changed by it.

connect

In your group, talk with each other about your first impressions of Mark. What connected most with you? How did you react to Jesus' teachings? Did reading Mark change your perspectives about the Bible or Jesus? Explain.

go deeper

Choose one of the key ideas you found while reading through Mark, and pray that God will give you wisdom to help you apply it to your life in the weeks to come. Write some of those specific prayers below,

Memory Verse of the Week

Did a particular verse make you think? Is there a verse you can't get out of your head? Write it down and memorize it. Allow God's Word to permanently brand itself in your head and your heart.

notes from group discussion

God has arrived

Lesson 2

The beginning of the gospel about Jesus Christ, the Son of God.

Mark 1:1

The Jews were tired of waiting for God's promises to come true. God had promised a messiah, someone who would deliver them from oppression and establish His kingdom, the nation of Israel. For four hundred years, Israel hadn't seen any sign that God was planning to keep His word.

To make matters worse, they were stuck under others' totalitarian rule: Greece, Persia, and Rome all took their turn ruling Palestine. But now, in Mark 1, their luck seems to be changing. A messenger from God has spoken up: "Prepare the way for the Lord" (verse 3).

Read the first chapter of Mark.

study

1 In your own words, explain John the Baptist's message.

Desert (1:3,12). It's interesting that John baptized in the desert, especially because the Jews viewed the desert as the place where evil spirits lived. Another thought: Jesus was tempted in the desert, where He was most certainly visited by an evil spirit.

fyi

Who was John? Luke tells us John was the son of Elizabeth, a relative of Jesus' mother, Mary.

fyi

Baptism. Jews often used baptism as a purification rite for Gentiles who converted to Judaism. But John went further, encouraging not only Gentiles to be baptized, but also Jews. For all, it was a sign of turning away from sin in preparation for the coming Messiah.

fyi

2 Read God's words of approval in verse 11. If your parents ever said something like this, what would it mean to you? What do you think it meant to Jesus?

3 Why do you think God's Spirit sent Jesus to suffer in the wilderness for forty days (1:12-13)?

The kingdom of God. You can't properly interpret the
Gospels without clearly understanding the concept of the

fyi

kingdom of God. The Jews were waiting for the Messiah and the
"age to come" through and in which God would defeat evildoers and
rule with peace, justice, health, and prosperity.

So when Jesus came, proving He was the Messiah, His disciples
thought the time of the kingdom of God was imminent. When He
died and rose again, the disciples thought this was Jesus' way of
finalizing the arrival of the kingdom.

However, after the Resurrection, the disciples soon realized Jesus
didn't bring the "finale," but the beginning of the end. This is where it
gets kind of confusing. The disciples realized that in a sense, because
Jesus came, died, and rose, and because He sent the Spirit, the kingdom had already come. But in another sense, Jesus wasn't finished,
and the kingdom was still *to* come. So it was *already* but *not yet.*

In this way, Jesus' second coming makes sense. The kingdom has
come, but not in its fullest capacity. Jesus has come, but He will
come again.

4 Try to get inside the minds of Simon, Andrew, James, and John.
Why would they drop everything and immediately follow Jesus
(1:18,20)? Do you think we should have that same urgency today?
Why, or why not?

5 What might it mean that Jesus taught "as one who had authority, not as the teachers of the law" (1:22)?

6 We know that Jesus often secluded Himself to pray and recharge (1:35). Why did He do this?

7 What does Jesus' interaction with the leper say about Jesus (1:40-45)?

8 From everything you've read so far, what are your thoughts on Jesus' character, ministry, and interactions with people?

9 The Jews expected their Messiah to be a warrior king, but things did not turn out as they anticipated. How has your experience with Jesus been different from what you expected?

connect

Discuss some of the unusual events in this chapter. For example, consider why the sinless Jesus had to be baptized by John. Did you notice who "drove" or pushed Jesus into the desert to do spiritual battle with Satan? What about the disciples who just quit their jobs to follow some stranger? That's not normal, is it? How do these things fit in with your ideas about spirituality or the way God works?

Then pray. Thank God for what you have learned and ask Him for wisdom to apply it in your life this week.

go deeper

For further study, read the Old Testament verses that Mark quotes in this chapter. Mark 1:2 is a direct quote from Malachi 3:1, and Mark 1:3 comes from Isaiah 40:3. In context, what are the Old Testament authors' main points? How do these original main points coincide with what Mark was trying to say?

Memory Verse of the Week

Did a particular verse make you think? Is there a verse you can't get out of your head? Write it down and memorize it. Allow God's Word to permanently brand itself in your head and your heart.

notes from group discussion

Jesus Christ, superstar

Lesson 3

"**Whoever** does God's will is my brother and sister and mother."

Mark 3:35

Mark 1 started off with a bang. Jesus, the miracle-worker, traveled around healing people and gathering more and more followers . . . so many that He couldn't go anywhere without a crowd surrounding Him. But with His popularity and power came opposition. The religious leaders hated Jesus because He challenged not only their authority but their whole way of life. Even Christ's family – His own mother! – thought He was out of control.

Yet as we know, Jesus had a divine purpose. Regardless of the opposition – or maybe because of it – Jesus was determined to bring a new way of life and love to the people He had created.

Read Mark 2:1–3:35.

1 When the paralytic's friends proved faithful, Jesus healed him (2:5,10-12). Why do you think their faith made such a difference?

Roof (2:4). How did the paralytic's friends lower him through a hole they made in a roof? Today we have insulated houses and sturdy roofs. But in the first-century Middle East, the roof of the average house was flat and made with wood beams covered with brushwood and clay. It would have been fairly easy for them to take the roof apart or make a hole in it.

fyi

2 Jesus healed the paralytic by saying, "Your sins are forgiven," and only later said, "Take your mat and go home," in other words, "You're healed" (2:5,11). Describe the difference between these two phrases. Why were the scribes so mad about it?

3 Why were people with bad reputations drawn to Jesus? Are they drawn to you? Why, or why not?

fyi *Tax collectors.* Romans hired these men to collect money for their empire, but most tax collectors were corrupt. They'd fulfill their quota with the Romans and collect tons of extra cash to keep for themselves. Jews considered tax collectors traitors.

fyi *Pharisees.* Although there weren't many of them (about 1 percent of the Jewish population), Pharisees earned respect—not necessarily approval—by creating a strict method of obedience to Moses' Law. Pharisees considered their rules, and themselves, just as authoritative as the Law itself.

4 Try to think like Pharisees. According to their worldview, why did they think it was a bad idea to hang out with sinners?

5 Why did Jesus hold the polar opposite belief?

6 We've now looked at five ways Jesus created conflict. What are they?

7 Summarize the religious leaders' reasons for opposing Him.

Apostle. This word comes from the Greek *apostello*, which means "to send." Apostles were sent out with full authority to act on behalf of Jesus.

fyi

8 Why do you think Jesus didn't want the demons to announce who He was (3:11-12)?

9 Jesus' family thought He was crazy (3:21). Why? Have people ever thought you were crazy for believing in Christ?

10 What is blasphemy "against the Holy Spirit"? Look at the context of verses 23-30 to help. What makes this sin worse than others?

11 What did Jesus mean when He said, "Whoever does God's will is my brother and sister and mother" (3:35)? Do you think He was too harsh with His family?

live

12 Can you think of a time when God called you to do something that seemed to conflict with your physical needs (2:23-28)? How did you respond? Do you think you responded correctly? Why or why not?

connect

Take turns talking about one thing you learned in this lesson that you didn't know before. Then close in prayer, thanking Jesus that He cares enough to confront us with areas in our lives where we need to be transformed by the gospel, not by rules. Pray that He reveals areas of potential renovation in your life.

go deeper

Jesus' call brought together former enemies like Matthew the tax collector and Simon the Zealot (3:16,18). How has Christ changed your attitudes toward people, or groups of people, with whom you previously did not associate? What changes in attitude still need to be made?

Memory Verse of the Week 🎧

Did a particular verse make you think? Is there a verse you can't get out of your head? Write it down and memorize it. Allow God's Word to permanently brand itself in your head and your heart.

notes from group discussion

Jesus Christ, storyteller

Again he said, "What shall we say the kingdom of God is like, or what parable shall we use to describe it? It is like a mustard seed, which is the smallest seed you plant in the ground. Yet when planted, it grows and becomes the largest of all garden plants, with such big branches that the birds of the air can perch in its shade."

Mark 4:30-32

You need to know the etymology of the word *parable* before we dive into this lesson. It comes from the Greek word *parabole,* which signifies something that is "set alongside" something else in order to make a comparison. For example, Jesus compares faith to a tiny mustard seed. As you read this passage (and the rest of Mark), you'll see that Jesus used parables all the time. He used them in the form of stories, riddles, even jokes. Jesus compared a difficult concept with something familiar so His listeners could better understand. Here are some things to keep in mind as you study parables:

- Parables are designed to focus on one central truth, not many truths. Unlike an allegory, not every detail of a parable has a relative (in this case, spiritual) meaning. The details of a parable aren't as important as the truth it conveys.

- Often parables call the listener or reader to a response. Always ask yourself, *How does the parable relate to me?*

- It's important to pay attention to the culture in which the parable was spoken (in this case, a first-century Palestinian farm community). To grasp the full meaning of the message, we as modern-day readers should be aware of cultural details.

- Parables communicate truth *indirectly.* They call listeners or readers to ponder the meaning, instead of just giving it away.

Read Mark 4:1-34.

1 The first time we see Jesus teaching in parables is right after His family questions His ministry. Do you think this timing is significant? Why, or why not?

The farmer. In those days, farmers sowed seed by scattering handfuls of it all over the ground (instead of in perfect rows like modern-day farmers do).

fyi

The path. This is where the farmer walked in the fields. That ground was packed so tightly, that a seed landing there stayed on the surface, where birds could eat it.

fyi

Rocky places. These were places where the soil was too shallow for the seed to develop roots. The seeds were easily scorched by the sun.

fyi

Thorns. Even if the farmer cut away thorny plants, their roots could grow back so quickly they'd choke out growth from seeds nearby.

fyi

2 The farmers to whom Jesus spoke would have been very familiar with the details of this parable. So why did Jesus assume the crowds wouldn't quite get it?

3 Jesus only explained the "secret" of this parable to His disciples. Why?

4 What is the "word" that the farmer sows? Explain why it is important.

5 We know that the Jews expected their Messiah to lead a political and cultural revolution. But it didn't exactly happen that way. Reflect on how Jesus' statements in 4:14-20 compare to their expectations of the kingdom. What are the obstacles Jesus says prevent people from accepting and living the gospel? List specific actions we might take to overcome these obstacles.

6 In the parable of the grain, verses 26-29, Jesus compared the growth of the kingdom to the slow, at times invisible, growth of a seed. Looking at your own life, how does this encourage or discourage you?

7 Review the parables and see if you can find a pattern to them. Do you think there's a reason for their order?

live

8 Looking back at each parable, write what stuck out to you. Did you find a specific application to each parable? Did you learn something new about Jesus or His followers? Did you find comparisons to your situations?

The parable of the sower

The parable of the grain

The parable of the mustard seed

9 Name one way you can apply these truths to your life this week.

connect

Discuss any questions you may have had during this lesson. After discussion, get into three groups, each representing a parable from this lesson, and spend time praying for Christians all over the world.

Sower group. Pray for those who believe, that they would become good soil and allow the Word to saturate their hearts and lives.

Grains group. Pray that believers would patiently dedicate themselves to "growing" in their relationship with God.

Mustard seed group. Pray for the growth of God's kingdom, that people all around the world would come to know Him.

go deeper

In the Jewish tradition, the coming of the kingdom of God would bring judgment as well as salvation. List and explain the references to judgment and salvation in Mark 4:3-32.

Memory Verse of the Week

Did a particular verse make you think? Is there a verse you can't get out of your head? Write it down and memorize it. Allow God's Word to permanently brand itself in your head and your heart.

notes from group discussion

the unexpected God

Lesson 5

He got up, rebuked the wind and said to the waves, "Quiet! Be still!" Then the wind died down and it was completely calm.

Mark 4:39

Jesus didn't do anything the way the Jews expected. He wasn't a glorious warrior king (in the way they had imagined). He taught spiritual messages in parables and espoused an unconventional ministry approach.

He even stretched the boundaries of Judaism by reaching out to the Gentiles. This was important because it clearly demonstrated that God's kingdom would not be restricted to one race or nation, but rather would be open to all who would turn from their sins and trust in Him.

Read Mark 4:35–5:43.

1 Contrast Jesus' behavior during the storm with the way His disciples reacted. What do you suppose the disciples learned about Him from this episode (4:37)?

Tombs. It made sense that a demon-possessed man lived in a tomb because of the popular belief that tombs were favorite haunts of demons.

fyi

Legion. A Roman legion consisted of approximately six thousand soldiers, so you get the picture of how many demons might have possessed that man.

fyi

Pigs. According to Moses' Law, pigs were unclean. The fact that there was such a large herd in that region shows that many Gentiles lived there.

fyi

Decapolis. This is the Greek word for "ten cities." It was a confederation of ten cities located mostly on the eastern shore of the Sea of Galilee.

fyi

2 Why did Jesus permit the demons to go into the pigs (5:11-13)?

3 Jesus did not allow the Gentile who had been possessed by demons to follow Him (5:19). Why?

4 Think about how the formerly possessed man reacted to Jesus' command (5:19). In what ways is this a good example for us?

fyi **Bleeding (5:25).** This woman was likely suffering from some kind of uterine disease. This was not only unhealthy and uncomfortable, but it also made her ceremonially unclean, which basically shut her off from worshiping God and being with her friends. Anyone whom she touched would have become unclean for a time.

5 Why do you think the woman was afraid to admit that she touched Jesus (5:33)?

6 Does His reply to her comfort you at all? If so, how?

7 Jairus's daughter is the first person Jesus raised from the dead. He only let five people witness the miracle and asked them not to spread the news. Does this tell you anything about Jesus' ministry? About Jesus' character? Explain.

58

8 Sometimes, by what He did, Jesus gave people a reason to have faith. Other times Jesus acted on the faith people already had. Write down a time when He gave you a reason to have faith. Then write down an instance when you believed, and because of it, Jesus responded.

9 What, if anything, did Jesus do or say in this section that has helped to increase your faith?

connect

Mark focuses heavily on the importance of faith in our walk with Christ. Discuss with your group what you learned about faith. Then pray. Ask God to increase your faith and give you opportunities to practice it.

Write down every instance in Mark 4:35–5:43 where faith and fear show up in the same story. What is the relationship between faith and fear? Elaborate.

Memory Verse of the Week

Did a particular verse make you think? Is there a verse you can't get out of your head? Write it down and memorize it. Allow God's Word to permanently brand itself in your head and your heart.

notes from group discussion

feeding the hungry

Lesson 6

When they saw him walking on the lake, they thought he was a ghost. They cried out, because they all saw him and were terrified. Immediately he spoke to them and said, "Take courage! It is I. Don't be afraid."

Mark 6:49-50

In these chapters, Jesus continued to amp up His ministry. Venturing into Gentile territory, He demonstrated the power of the kingdom of God everywhere He went. As He did so, He attacked the powers of darkness, proving His supremacy over evil and death.

Jesus also proved that He is the Lord over all creation (including food!) and because of His great demonstrations of power, people flocked from everywhere to catch a glimpse. Yet, even though they saw all these signs, many still lacked faith.

Read Mark 6:1–8:26.

1 What prevented Jesus from doing more than a few miracles in Nazareth (6:5-6)? Why do you think that made such a difference?

2 Jesus sent the apostles out "two by two" on their mission (6:7). He also told them to travel light. Why do you think He did these two things?

3 People had many things to say about Jesus—but most of them did not say He was the Messiah (6:14-15). What was it about Jesus' ministry that kept people from believing in who He really was?

4 In executing John the Baptist, Herod killed a man he greatly respected (6:20). What do his motivation and his action say about the way sin operates?

Eight months of a man's wages (6:37). This literally means "two hundred denarii." A denarius was the daily wage for a hired hand.

Loaves (6:38). These were barley loaves (we know because of John 6:9). They were small and flat, and people would eat several of them in one meal.

5   What does Jesus' reaction to the crowd of five thousand (6:34) tell us about . . .

His character?

His mission?

6   Why do you think He gave them way more than they needed?

7   Mark makes it clear that if the disciples understood what happened when Jesus fed the five thousand, they wouldn't have been surprised that He walked on water or calmed the wind. By learning about all these events, what can we understand about Jesus?

fyi   *Tradition of the elders (7:3,5).* Although this oral tradition was not even written down yet (not until AD 200), the Pharisees and scribes considered it to be as binding as the Law of Moses itself. It was formulated by rabbis to help people apply Moses' Law to specific life situations.

Corban (7:11). The Corban was one such tradition. It stated that a man could declare a portion of his wealth to be dedicated to God. Jesus spoke to the abuse of this rule because people were designating money they didn't actually have and never intended to give.

8 How did Jesus view the authority of the Law of Moses (7:10,19)?

9 In light of this, what authority should Christians give to the Old Testament?

10 Do you see any connection between the way Jesus acted in this section (7:24-37) and His teaching in the previous section (7:1-23)? Explain your answer.

Another large crowd (8:1). Most of the people in this crowd were Gentiles. We know this because Mark 7:24–8:10 explains how Jesus did the same sort of miracles in Gentile territory that He did among the Jews.

11 What does the disciples' response to Jesus in 8:4 tell us about their faith?

fyi *Sign from heaven (8:11).* The Pharisees weren't actually asking for miracles, but they wanted proof that Jesus was the Messiah (see Daniel 7:13). Again Jesus did things differently than anyone expected, and because of that, the Pharisees disbelieved.

12 Yeast is used in baking bread, in making it rise. In rabbinical writings, it was usually a symbol for evil. Considering the Pharisees' demand for a sign from heaven (8:11) and their view of the kingdom of God, what do you think Jesus meant when He spoke of the "yeast of the Pharisees" (8:15)?

13 Jesus gradually restored the blind man's sight after He twice asked the disciples, "Do you still not understand [who I am]?" (8:17,21). Is there a connection between the multistep healing of the blind man and the disciples' slowness to understand Jesus? Do you see any implications of this principle in your own life? Explain.

live

14 No two healings of Jesus recorded by Mark were exactly alike. How is this relevant to the way Jesus deals with us? How does it relate, if at all, to the way you represent Jesus to others.

15 What recurring themes about Jesus did you notice in this section (6:1–8:26) and what new truths did you learn?

connect

Talk with each other about what you think kept the disciples from recognizing who Jesus was. Discuss barriers that keep us from trusting Jesus today. Then spend time in worshipful prayer, praising Jesus for His patience and grace.

go deeper

Review every instance in Mark 1–6 when Jesus or His disciples cast out demons. What does this activity tell us about the purpose behind His ministry?

Memory Verse of the Week

Did a particular verse make you think? Is there a verse you can't get out of your head? Write it down and memorize it. Allow God's Word to permanently brand itself in your head and your heart.

notes from group discussion

Jesus' true identity

Lesson 7

"**For** whoever wants to save his life will lose it, but whoever loses his life for me and for the gospel will save it."

Mark 8:35

As time went on, Jesus became more straightforward about who He was and what He came to do. Crowds still rushed to see Him, but they were more interested in a spectacle than in life-change.

Jesus did reveal His true identity—that He was the Messiah—but He still kept that fact within His closest circle: His disciples. Even still, they struggled with faith. Though they believed in Him, they didn't know exactly what to believe. Jesus continued to teach them about the kingdom of God and to prepare them for ministry. He knew that soon enough He would have to leave them and return to heaven.

Read Mark 8:27–10:12.

study

1 Why do you think Jesus waited until this point in His ministry to reveal Himself as Messiah? Why did He ask His disciples not to tell anyone else?

2 Why did Jesus say, "Get behind me, Satan!" to Peter (8:33)? Sounds pretty harsh, doesn't it? What do "Satan" and the "things of men" have in common?

Take up his cross (8:34-38). Under Roman law, a criminal was condemned to carry his own cross to the execution site. So, when Jesus tells His disciples to carry their crosses and follow Him, He is providing a poignant analogy for a life of following Him.

Soul (8:36). Jews considered the soul to be more than just someone's intangible spirit, but his or her entire life—body, mind, and spirit.

The kingdom of God come with power (9:1). Some scholars think Jesus is referring to His second coming here. Others think He is referring to the coming of the Holy Spirit at Pentecost (see Acts 2:1-21). Either way, all three Synoptic Gospels (remember, that's all but John) link this saying with the Transfiguration account (9:2-13), which makes it probable that the writers consider this event, at least in part, a fulfillment of this saying.

Cloud (9:7). In the Old Testament, a cloud was a sign of God's presence and glory.

3   Elijah and Moses were extremely important to first-century Jewish thought. Elijah represented the Prophets and Moses represented the Law – the two main divisions of Jewish scripture. Why would God choose those two men to appear with Jesus (9:1-8)?

4   Why were the disciples afraid to ask Jesus about His death and resurrection (9:32)? How do you think you would have reacted?

5   What might have prompted the disciples' fight about which of them was "the greatest" (9:33-34)?

fyi   *Servant (9:35).* This Greek word does not mean merely a slave or hired hand, but someone who serves a king. The same word is used when Paul speaks of "deacons" or "ministers."

6   Jesus defined greatness as being a servant. What are some examples from your life of serving "in Jesus' name"?

7   Explain Jesus' reaction to the disciples in 9:39-41.

Hell (9:43). The Greek word for hell refers to a place south of Jerusalem called the Valley of Hinnom. This valley was used for burning the city's garbage, and its fires never went out. Because of that, it became known as a symbol for a place of divine punishment.

fyi

8   As He urges His followers to avoid sin, Jesus uses some harsh language. Why?

Certificate of divorce (10:4). This refers to Deuteronomy 24:1, where Moses says that a man can divorce his wife if he finds something indecent about her. Depending on the rabbinical interpretation, it could mean anything from a wife's immoral act to burning her husband's breakfast!

fyi

If she divorces her husband (10:12). Jesus recognized the legal right of a woman to divorce her husband, a right not recognized in Judaism at that time.

fyi

9 In the Old Testament, salt represented purification (it was commonly used to keep meat from spoiling). To help make sense of Jesus' metaphor in 9:50, write down other characteristics of salt and how they could possibly apply here.

10 When Jesus asked the Pharisees, "What did Moses *command* you?" they replied, "Moses *permitted . . .* " (10:3-4, emphasis added). Explain the significance of this difference.

11 In your own words, summarize Jesus' view of marriage.

live

12 Jesus said, "Whoever is not against us is for us" (9:40). How can you apply this to your life when you think about the world around you? Different church denominations? Your school campus? Your family?

13 What truths from this lesson connected with you? Make a plan to apply one of them this week, either in your prayer life or by acting on a specific situation.

connect

This week, share ideas for how your group might more effectively pray for each other's needs. Then pray that God would give you better understanding of how you can live out the radical gospel of Jesus Christ within the context of your social life, your school, your family.

go deeper

Compare these two accounts of Peter's confession of Christ: Mark 8:27-30 and Matthew 16:13-20. Write the truths from Matthew's account that Mark doesn't mention.

Memory Verse of the Week

Did a particular verse make you think? Is there a verse you can't get out of your head? Write it down and memorize it. Allow God's Word to permanently brand itself in your head and your heart.

notes from group discussion

on the way
to the cross

"**The** Son of Man will be betrayed to the chief priests and teachers of the law. They will condemn him to death and will hand him over to the Gentiles, who will mock him and spit on him, flog him and kill him. Three days later he will rise."

Mark 10:33-34

Jesus consistently warned His disciples that following Him would not bring worldly greatness. Instead following Him would most certainly result in pain, in persecution – at least on earth. The gospel of the kingdom of God didn't look much like good news.

But regardless of what the disciples expected or wanted, they finally learned the full truth about Jesus' calling. They began to sense that they were uncomfortably close to something terrible. They also started to understand that their Savior was a "suffering servant," not a warrior king. (Yes, after all this time with Jesus, they still had messed-up expectations. Don't we all?)

As Jesus neared Jerusalem, He didn't do much teaching. He was focused on His monumental mission: the Cross.

Read Mark 10:13–11:33.

1 Why were Jesus' disciples so "amazed" when He said it was hard for a rich man to enter God's kingdom?

The rich (10:23). Back in New Testament times, if you were rich it was considered proof that you were blessed by heaven.

fyi

2 What prompted Jesus to respond to Peter the way He did in 10:29?

3 When Jesus predicted His death and resurrection for a third time in 10:32-34, what new information did He add (see 8:31; 9:31)? Why do you think He included this?

4 What did Jesus mean when He talked about the "cup" and the "baptism" (10:38)?

fyi ***Ransom for many (10:45).*** In Greek, the word *ransom* referred to the price paid to liberate a slave.

fyi ***Son of David (10:47).*** The Jews of Jesus' day thought the Messiah would be from the line of David the king. When Bartimaeus called Jesus "Son of David," he was implying his belief in Jesus as the Messiah.

5 Bartimaeus was persistent with Jesus, repeatedly calling Him to respond (10:46-52). What does his adamancy tell us about the way we can approach Jesus in prayer?

6 Jesus requested a colt (or donkey) that had never been ridden before because unridden animals were used for especially sacred purposes. Still, it's important to note that He chose a donkey, not a warhorse. Read Zechariah 9:9 to understand the public statement Jesus made by riding a donkey into Jerusalem. Explain the significance in your own words.

fyi ***Hosanna! (11:9).*** By spreading cloaks and branches, the Jews were showing royal honor to Jesus. And by shouting hosanna (which in Hebrew means "save now"), they were repeating the message of Psalm 118:25, which just happened to be the psalm reserved for the Messiah's arrival. In the same way, "Blessed is he who comes in the name of the LORD" is quoted from Psalm 118:26.

7 What does the crowd's reaction tell you about how *they* interpreted Jesus' entry into Jerusalem (11:9-10)?

8 Some people interpret the Bible to mean that the cursing of the fig tree is a real-life happening (11:12-14,20-25). Considering fig trees were sometimes used to represent Israel, what point was Jesus trying to make?

9 How are verses 11:22-25 relevant to your own experience of prayer?

Buying and selling (11:15). Many Jews assembled in Jerusalem for Passover, but it was often impossible for them to bring along the animals required for sacrifice. Because of this, cattle, lambs, birds, and other animals were sold in the "court of the Gentiles." This was an area just outside the temple that Gentiles could enter, but that's as far as they could go. Jesus demonstrated, through His anger, that the place where the Gentiles worshiped was just as valuable to Him as the inner courts.

fyi

10 Whose authority did Jesus challenge when He drove the money-changers out of the temple area (11:15-18)? What statement did He make about His own authority?

11 Both the cursing of the fig tree and the clearing of the temple tell us about Jesus' attitude toward the spiritual condition of the Israelites. How can you apply the events in the Gentiles' court to Christians today?

12 Why do you think Jesus didn't answer the religious leaders' questions directly, but instead returned their questions with a question of his own (11:27-33)?

live

Jesus cursed a fig tree that looked beautiful from a distance but bore no fruit. Ask God to show you one specific area of your life that may seem spiritually mature at first glance, but where you have yet to bear significant fruit. Then ask God to show you ways you can bear fruit in that area. Write them down here.

connect

This lesson has focused on the beginning of the final week of Jesus' life. In your group, discuss the elements of this beginning (the triumphal entry, the cursing of the fig tree, the clearing of the temple, and so on) and how they fit within the scope of the entire week.

go deeper

Compare Mark's reference to Jesus as a "ransom for many" (10:45) with the following passages. What do these passages tell you about your relationship with Jesus?

Isaiah 53:5-6

Romans 5:6-8,15-19

1 Corinthians 15:3

2 Corinthians 5:21

Hebrews 9:15

Memory Verse of the Week 🎧

Did a particular verse make you think? Is there a verse you can't get out of your head? Write it down and memorize it. Allow God's Word to permanently brand itself in your head and your heart.

notes from group discussion

nonconformity

Lesson 9

"**I** tell you the truth, this poor widow has put more into the treasury than all the others. They all gave out of their wealth; but she, out of her poverty, put in everything – all she had to live on."

Mark 12:43-44

You'd think that by now the religious leaders, the Jews, and even the disciples would get it – that they would understand Jesus' message. Jesus didn't come to judge Gentiles and justify Israel, but rather to judge Israel for her hypocrisy and to call people to a true obedience, a true faith. Jesus didn't come to preach the love of worldly power, wealth, and beauty, but a love of God and of others.

In these final days, Jesus still tries to get His disciples to realize this truth: Don't conform to the present age, but put your faith in what's to come, when God's kingdom will be fully established. These words are as important today as they were two thousand years ago.

Read Mark 12:1–13:37.

1 In the parable of the tenants (12:1-12) . . .

To whom is Jesus talking to?

Whom do the farmers represent?

Whom do the servants represent?

Who is the "son" in verse 6?

Who are the "others" in verse 9?

2 Explain the meaning of this parable in your own words.

3 In verses 10-11, Jesus quotes Psalm 118:22-23. What is the significance of saying He will fulfill this psalm?

4 When the Pharisees and Herodians asked Jesus if one should pay taxes to Caesar, He gave what seemed like a vague answer. How do you interpret what He said?

fyi *Seven brothers (12:20).* This absurd little story may have been a joke the Sadducees used to embarrass their more popular rivals, the Pharisees, who did believe in the resurrection.

5 According to Jesus, the Sadducees did not know two things: the Scriptures and the power of God (12:24). What about these things didn't they know?

6 What did the teacher of the law mean when he said that loving God and our neighbors is worth more than offerings and sacrifices? Why did Jesus then say, "You are not far from the kingdom of God" (12:34)?

7 Many people think that the really big sins are things like sexual promiscuity or drug use. What really big sins does Jesus point out in 12:38-40? Why are these sins so serious?

8 What was significant about the poor widow's offering? Why did Jesus go out of His way to call attention to it (12:43)?

9 Jesus was quick to turn the disciples' observance of beautiful architecture into a discussion about the end times. What was His main reason for doing so (13:5)?

fyi *Abomination that causes desolation (13:14).* This phrase comes from the book of Daniel, where it occurs four times. One of the occurrences clearly refers to the destruction of the temple. The other three are not so easy to interpret, but many scholars argue that two are references to the end times. It's also hard to say whether Mark 13:14 refers to events before the fall of Jerusalem in AD 70, or before the end of the age just prior to Christ's return. It's probably best to read the statement openly, allowing it to be a double fulfillment.

The elect (13:20). In the New Testament, "the elect" means not just Israel as a nation but all true believers in Christ.

10 What one thing *must* happen before Christ comes again (13:10)? What does that mean for us today?

This generation (13:30). There is a lot of controversy over what Jesus meant when He said, "This generation will certainly not pass away until all these things have happened." It is hard to know if Jesus was saying that the calamities leading up to His second coming would all happen within the generation of His followers, if only some would happen, or if *generation* meant something different from a thirty-year period. But that's not the point of this passage. Jesus is not concerned about predicting when He'll return. He wants to warn His disciples that they will have to go through very tough times before He returns.

11 Jesus said that during the end times, Christians will be tempted to follow false christs and false prophets. He said these men and women will perform miracles to deceive the elect. What does "if that were possible" mean (Matthew 24:24)?

12 Why do you think God has chosen not to reveal when Christ will return (Mark 13:32)?

13 What's your impression of Jesus after reading chapters 12 and 13? What do you observe about His personality, His abilities, and His preaching?

live

Think about ways we, as Christians, need to "be alert" and "watch" (13:33,37). Ask God to help you obey these commands of Jesus.

14 How do you think the disciples would have responded if Jesus had told them He wouldn't return for at least two thousand years? What do you think about Jesus' "soon" return?

connect

In your group, discuss times when you lacked faith in either the Scriptures or the power of God. Perhaps this has even occurred during your study of Mark. (Just like the disciples, we all struggle with faith sometimes, no matter how much time we spend with Jesus.) Then pray that God would give each person courage to trust Him in those areas.

go deeper

For further study, read the following passages and write about why New Testament writers make such a big effort to warn us about accumulating wealth.

Matthew 6:19-24

Luke 12:15-21

1 Timothy 6:7-10

How do these passages convict you or support the way you live your life now?

Memory Verse of the Week

Did a particular verse make you think? Is there a verse you can't get out of your head? Write it down and memorize it. Allow God's Word to permanently brand itself in your head and your heart.

notes from group discussion

the last meal

Lesson 10

While they were eating, Jesus took bread, gave thanks and broke it, and gave it to his disciples, saying, "Take it; this is my body." Then he took the cup, gave thanks and offered it to them, and they all drank from it. "This is my blood of the covenant, which is poured out for many."

Mark 14:22-24

Jesus had already told His disciples about the future. Now it was time for the realities of those words to set in. He met one last time with His disciples as a group, was betrayed by one of those disciples, and finally faced the powers of darkness (not only Satan, but also the religious leaders of Jerusalem). In some ways, the religious leaders' actions suggested they understood Jesus' message better than His own disciples did. Perhaps the Pharisees knew He would end their religion as they knew it.

Jesus understood that His sufferings on the cross would open the way for His glorious return, so He did not resist the fore-known outcome of the Crucifixion. In what may be one of the greatest ironies of all time, the religious leaders, Pilate, and even Jesus' disciples actually thought His death would put an end to this whole business of His being the "Messiah." Little did they know it was all part of God's plan.

Read Mark 14:1–15:15.

study

fyi

Passover (14:1). In Exodus 12:1-30, an angel of the LORD killed all the firstborn sons of Egyptians but "passed over" the homes of Israelites who were captives in Egypt. The Israelites were told to sacrifice a pure, unblemished lamb and put its blood on the sides and tops of their doors. The angel would pass over any door with this mark. The Passover meal was and still is a major Israelite holiday because it commemorated this pivotal event in their history. The Feast of Unleavened Bread followed Passover and lasted seven days.

fyi

A woman (14:3). This woman was likely Mary, sister of Martha and Lazarus, the man whom Jesus raised from the dead.

fyi

Some of those present (14:4). Matthew 26:8 tells us that it was Jesus' disciples who were indignant.

1   What does Jesus' anointing tell us about the disciples' understanding of who He was and why He came (14:3-9)? How do you think you would have responded?

2   None of the Gospels tells us precisely why Judas betrayed Jesus (14:10-11). Was it only for the money? Why else would Judas do this?

fyi *A man carrying a jar of water (14:13).* This was very unusual because women normally carried the water jars.

fyi *A large upper room, furnished and ready (14:15).* Just as He did for His triumphal entry into Jerusalem, Jesus had prepared this event in advance. This suggests that He had a circle of disciples in the greater Jerusalem area in addition to the twelve disciples.

fyi *Blood of the covenant (14:24).* Forgiveness of sins under the Old Covenant—the Law of Moses—required a blood sacrifice. As a New Testament writer put it, "Without the shedding of blood there is no forgiveness" (Hebrews 9:22).

3 In traditional Passover services, the central emphasis of the meal is on the sacrificial lamb, which is served with unleavened bread (called matzoth), bitter herbs, and wine. But Jesus' meal was a little different. Where did *He* place the emphasis (14:22-24)? Why did He do this?

4 What promise did Jesus make to His disciples in verse 25? Write down its significance.

5 How do you relate to Peter's insistence that he would not disown Jesus (14:29,31)?

Abba (14:36; Romans 8:15; Galatians 4:6). This was an Aramaic word for father, but it was an intimate expression, kind of like our word *daddy*. The Jews did not use this word, because they thought it was too informal and irreverent. Jesus not only used it, but Paul also encourages us to do so.

fyi

6 We know that God did not grant Jesus' request of "taking this cup from me" (14:36). Why not? What does this teach us about prayer?

7 Why did the religious leaders bring a large, armed crowd to arrest Jesus (14:43,48)? Infer something about their intentions and understanding of Jesus.

8   Put yourself at the scene of His arrest. Only minutes earlier, Jesus was "overwhelmed with sorrow to the point of death" (14:34). Yet when He was betrayed, He stayed calm. How was Jesus able to handle the moment of crisis with courage, while His followers were not?

fyi   *Sanhedrin (14:55).* This was the high court of Jerusalem, composed of the chief priests and other religious leaders. If all the members were present, there would have been seventy of them. What's interesting is that nighttime gatherings of the Sanhedrin were highly unusual and possibly even illegal. This demonstrates not only that the religious leaders were quick to make exceptions to rules, but also that they had contempt for Jesus. The trial itself was also unusual because it was a chaotic meeting of false witnesses and no real opportunity for a defense on Jesus' part. Whether or not this was illegal, it was certainly not fair.

9   Why do you think Jesus initially didn't answer the charges brought against Him in 14:61? Why did He choose to answer the high priest's question in 14:62?

10 Read Peter's denial (14:66-72). What is your reaction?

Pilate (15:1). Pontius Pilate was the Roman governor of fyi
Judea from AD 26 to 36. The Jews brought Jesus to him
because they could not legally put someone to death without his
approval (except in cases where the sanctity of the temple was
violated).

Flogged (15:15). Flogging was not a light beating; it was fyi
horrific. The whip used in flogging consisted of several pieces
of leather, onto which were tied pieces of metal and bone. The Jews
"mercifully" limited flogging to a maximum of forty whips, but the
Romans didn't have any such limitations. In many cases, victims of
Roman floggings did not survive. Pilate apparently had Jesus flogged
in a last-ditch effort to elicit mercy from the crowd so they would free
Jesus.

live

11 Have you ever been betrayed or abandoned by a friend? Knowing how it feels, how does it help you relate to Jesus? On the flip side, how does it help you to know that Jesus can relate to your pain?

12 In the space below (or in a separate journal), write about your reaction to this lesson. Think about your relationship with Jesus and how this study affects it.

connect

Here's something a little different. Arrange a time to celebrate the Lord's Supper as a group. You can have a communion session, or you can go all out by researching and preparing a traditional Jewish Passover service (called a seder). Either way, take the time to acknowledge together what Jesus did for all of us.

go deeper

For further study, compare the four gospel accounts of Judas. Then do the following: Make a list of factors you see—whether in Judas's personality, beliefs, or circumstances—that might have contributed to his decision to betray Jesus. Then look at your list and think about whether any of these factors might be inhibiting your own walk with Jesus.

Memory Verse of the Week

Did a particular verse make you think? Is there a verse you can't get out of your head? Write it down and memorize it. Allow God's Word to permanently brand itself in your head and your heart.

notes from group discussion

the best worst day

Lesson 11

And they crucified him.

Mark 15:24

It couldn't have been more depressing. For those who followed Jesus, this dark day showed no hope that He was ushering in the promised kingdom. Even the religious leaders of Israel and the rulers of Rome noticed the unusually dark skies. Jesus' own people had rejected Him, condemning Him to a death He didn't deserve.

Adding insult to injury, the way Jesus was crucified seemed to be final proof that He couldn't have been the Messiah – after all, God's own law said that anyone hung on a tree was under God's curse.

But in the end, God proved the opposite was true. Through Christ's death on the cross, God lifted Him up above all kings, all rulers, all people. Jesus became the name above all names, worthy of the worship of everything in, above, and below the earth.

Read Mark 15:16-47.

1 How is the soldier's treatment of Jesus a picture of the way people tend to treat God (15:16-20)?

2 Look at the way Jesus responded to them (He didn't strike them dead for their contempt). What does this say about God?

Cross. The cross consisted of two parts: a sturdy timber planted into the ground at the crucifixion site and a heavy crossbeam that was carried to the site strapped to the soon-to-be-victim's shoulders. Jesus was so weak from the flogging and other maltreatment that the soldiers had to enlist Simon into service.

fyi

Wine mixed with myrrh (15:23). This mixture was used as a narcotic to lessen pain. It seems very strange that a Roman soldier would have prepared this mixture, because they weren't known to be considerate of victims. It makes more sense that Jews had prepared the painkiller, maybe as a consolation to Jesus.

fyi

3 If you were Simon, how do you think you would have felt helping Jesus carry His cross?

4   The crucifixion process was agonizing – the most cruel and hideous punishment possible. After being beaten half to death, Jesus was nailed to the cross. Considering the time and pain that went into Jesus' crucifixion, why do you think Mark understated the account by simply writing, "And they crucified him" (15:24)?

fyi *Third, sixth, and ninth hour (15:25,33).* The third hour was around nine o'clock in the morning, which makes the sixth hour noon and the ninth hour three o'clock.

fyi *Written notice (15:26).* Each criminal's cross displayed a sign proclaiming his crime in large letters. This sign was attached to each cross, serving as a warning to anyone who would repeat the crime.

5   Read Psalm 22. Write down every reference (whether obvious or implied) to this psalm in Mark's account of the Crucifixion.

6   After reading this psalm, why do you think Jesus quoted Psalm 22:1 for all to hear (15:34)?

7 Why didn't Jesus answer the religious leaders' challenge to save Himself?

8 Jesus cried out in a loud voice twice before He died (15:34,37). Explain what you think Jesus meant in verse 34.

The curtain of the temple (15:38). In the temple were two areas: the Holy Place and the Most Holy Place. Priests were allowed in the Holy Place any time they wanted, but they could only enter the Most Holy Place once a year to make a sacrifice (on the Jewish holiday Yom Kippur). The curtain that separated those two holy places tore in two when Jesus died. It's obvious that it happened supernaturally, because (1) it was made of very heavy material and wasn't easily torn, and (2) it was torn straight down from top to bottom. This didn't happen just because God liked special effects; He did this to show everyone that Jesus' death gives direct access to God.

9 The centurion believed in Jesus because of "how he died" (15:39). What do you think Mark meant when he wrote that statement?

10 Mark tells us that Joseph, not only a high-ranking official but also a man of integrity, showed courage in asking for Jesus' body (15:43). Compare his actions to those of Christ's disciples.

live

11 When you think about "how Jesus died" (15:39) and the whole account of His death, how does it affect you?

12 How can you apply your response to Christ's death to your life this week?

connect

In your group, discuss the intensity of the whole crucifixion account. Openly talk about the emotions you feel (or the lack thereof) and the knowledge you've gained. Then pray with each other, spending the entire time praising Jesus for the work He did on the cross. Allow anyone to blurt out praises when they come to mind.

go deeper

To increase your understanding of Jesus' death, read all four Gospel accounts. Then write below where they match and where they diverge (what's added in some, what's subtracted in others).

Matthew 26:36–27:65

Luke 22:39–23:56

John 18:1–19:42

Which gospel account affects you most? Why?

Memory Verse of the Week

Did a particular verse make you think? Is there a verse you can't get out of your head? Write it down and memorize it. Allow God's Word to permanently brand itself in your head and your heart.

notes from group discussion

and then everything changed

"**You** are looking for Jesus the Nazarene, who was crucified. He has risen! He is not here."

Mark 16:6

Jesus' disciples were broken up when He died. They scattered all over the place like scared sheep. The only people who stood by Him were His mom, John, and some Galilean women who had taken care of Him during His ministry.

Some of the women were so devoted to Jesus that after He died, they went to anoint His dead body in the tomb. But they forgot one minor detail: the stone that covered the entrance was way too big for them to move. Thankfully, they didn't have to figure out how to move the stone because it was already pushed aside. And there was another surprise: they couldn't anoint Jesus' body, because it wasn't there.

Everything Jesus had promised was coming true. His life, death, and resurrection changed everything.

Read Mark 16:1-20.

1 Compare the way the disciples reacted at Jesus' arrest with the way the Galilean women reacted to Jesus' death (14:50; 16:1). Write down the possible motives of both groups.

A young man dressed in a white robe (16:5). The way this young man dressed tells us he was probably an angel. Matthew 28:2-3 validates this belief.

2 Why do you think the angel told the women to give a message to the "disciples *and Peter*" (16:7, emphasis added)?

3 Why did Jesus appear to Mary Magdalene first (16:1-7)?

4 How do you react to the way Jesus' disciples responded each time someone told them He had risen from the dead?

Whoever believes and is baptized (16:16). Baptism was considered a public display of faith in Christ, just as it is today. Back in the early church, belief in Jesus and baptism were inseparable — they were practically a single act.

5 Why does Jesus emphasize a public declaration of faith in Mark 16:16?

6 Think about Jesus' words in this verse. Does it make you think about the way you talk about Jesus with others? Does it scare you? Does it comfort you? Write your personal reaction to His statement.

7 What do you think *saved* means?

These signs (16:17-18). The signs that Jesus talks about here didn't happen very often in the New Testament (except the casting out of demons, which we've seen numerous times throughout this study). Also, not all these signs are alike. Some of them deal with active ministry and others are about God's protection. It's important to make the distinction between signs we should actively seek out and those God provides on a case-by-case basis. Otherwise we run the risk of abusing these promises (like playing with snakes and drinking their venom just because we think we're protected).

8 What is the significance of Jesus' ascension into heaven (16:19)? Why does it matter to us today?

live

How has studying Mark affected your view of Jesus? Reflect in prayer on what you've learned, and ask Jesus to transform your heart and your life.

connect

Talk about what you can do as individuals and as a group to obey Jesus' "great commission" to go into all the world and preach the good news (16:15-18). Then pray, thanking God for speaking to us through Mark. Ask the Holy Spirit to guide each of you in how you live, serve, and preach Jesus' good news.

go deeper

Think more about Jesus' resurrection. What did it accomplish for you? Read and respond to the following verses:

Romans 5:10

Romans 6:1-14

Romans 8:11

1 Corinthians 15:12-22

Memory Verse of the Week

Did a particular verse make you think? Is there a verse you can't get out of your head? Write it down and memorize it. Allow God's Word to permanently brand itself in your head and your heart.

notes from group discussion

study resources

It's true that studying the Bible can often lead you to answers for life's tough questions. But Bible study also prompts plenty of *new* questions. Perhaps you're intrigued by a passage and want to understand it better. Maybe you're stumped about what a particular verse or word means. Where do you go from here? Study resources can help. Research a verse's history, cultural context, and connotations. Look up unfamiliar words. Track down related Scripture passages elsewhere in the Bible. Study resources can help sharpen your knowledge of God's Word.

Below you'll find a selected bibliography of study resources. Use them to discover more, dig deeper, and ultimately grow closer to God.

historical and background sources

D. A. Carson, Douglas Moo, Leon Morris. *An Introduction to the New Testament.* Grand Rapids, Michigan: Zondervan, 1992.

Provides an overview of the New Testament for students and teachers. Covers historical and biographical information and includes outlines and discussions of each book's theological importance.

James I. Packer, Merrill C. Tenney, William White, Jr. *The Bible Almanac.* Nashville: Nelson, 1980.

Contains information about people of the Bible and how they lived. Photos and illustrations help the characters come to life.

Merrill C. Tenney. *New Testament Survey.* Grand Rapids, Mich.: Eerdmans, 1985.

Analyzes social, political, cultural, economic, and religious backgrounds of each New Testament book.

concordances, dictionaries, and atlases

concordances

If you are studying a specific word and want to know where to find it in the Bible, use a concordance. A concordance lists every verse in the Bible in which that word shows up. An *exhaustive* concordance includes every word in a given translation (there are different concordances for different Bible translations) and an *abridged* or *complete* concordance leaves out some words, some occurrences of the words, or both. Multiple varieties exist, so choose for yourself which one you like best. *Strong's Exhaustive Concordance* and *Young's Analytical Concordance of the Bible* are the most popular.

bible dictionaries

Sometimes called a *Bible encyclopedia,* a Bible dictionary alphabetically lists articles about people, places, doctrines, important words, customs, and geography of the Bible. Here are a few to consider:

The New Strong's Expanded Dictionary of Bible Words. Nashville: Nelson, 2001.

Defines more than 14,000 words. In addition, it includes an index that gives meanings of the word in the original language.

Nelson's New Illustrated Bible Dictionary. Nashville: Nelson, 1996.

Includes over 500 photos, maps, and pronunciation guides.

The New Unger's Bible Dictionary. Wheaton, Ill.: Moody, 1988.

Displays pictures, maps, and illustrations. Clearly written, easy to understand, and compatible with most Bible translations.

Vine's Expository Dictionary of New Testament Words. Peabody, Mass.: Hendrickson, 1993.

Lists major words and defines each New Testament Greek word.

bible atlases

We often skim over mentions of specific locations in the Bible, but location is an important element to understanding the context of a passage. A Bible atlas can help you understand the geography in a book of the Bible and how it may have affected the recorded events. Here are two good choices:

The Illustrated Bible Atlas. Grand Rapids, Mich.: Kregel, 1999.
Provides concise (and colorful) information on lands and cities where events took place. Includes historical notes.

The Carta Bible Atlas. Jerusalem, Israel: Carta, 2003.
Includes analytical notes on biblical events, military campaigns, travel routes, archeological highlights, as well as indexes. A very popular atlas for students, scholars, and clergy.

for small-group leaders

If you are the leader of a small group, or would like to lead a small group, these resources may help.

Ann Beyerlein. *Small Group Leaders' Handbook.* Downer's Grove, Ill.: InterVarsity, 1995.
Teaches biblical basis and growth stages of small groups. Helps leaders develop skills for resolving conflict, leading discussion, and planning for the future.

Laurie Polich. *Help! I'm a Small-Group Leader.* Grand Rapids, Mich.: Zondervan, 1998.
Offers tips and solutions to help you nurture your small group and accomplish your goals. Suggests techniques and questions to use in many Bible study circumstances.

Neal F. McBride. *How to Lead Small Groups.* Colorado Springs, Colo.: NavPress, 1990.

> *Covers leadership skills for all kinds of small groups. Filled with step-by-step guidance and practical exercises focusing on the most important aspects of small-group leadership.*

bible study methods

Tim LaHaye. *How to Study the Bible for Yourself.* Eugene, Ore.: Harvest House, 1998.

> *Teaches how to illuminate Scripture through study. Gives methods for understanding the Bible's major principles, promises, commands, key verses, and themes.*

Gordon Fee and Douglas Stuart. *How to Read the Bible for All It's Worth.* Grand Rapids, Mich.: Zondervan, 2003.

> *Offers chapters on interpreting and applying the different kinds of writing in the Bible: Epistles, Gospels, Old Testament Law, Old Testament narrative, the Prophets, Psalms, Wisdom, and Revelation. Also includes suggestions for commentaries on each book of the Bible.*

Oletta Wald. *The New Joy of Discovery in Bible Study.* Minneapolis: Augsburg, 2002.

> *Helps students of Scripture discover how to observe all that is in a text, how to ask questions of a text, and how to use grammar and passage structure to see the writer's point. Teaches methods for independent Bible study.*